A Brave Dog

by Claudia Doyle
illustrated by Merrill Rainey

Practice Decodable 80

McGraw Hill Education

Bothell, WA • Chicago, IL • Columbus, OH • New York, NY

MHEonline.com

Send all inquiries to:
McGraw-Hill Education
8787 Orion Place
Columbus, OH 43240-4027

ISBN: 978-0-02-133644-9
MHID: 0-02-133644-X

Printed in China.

8 9 10 11 12 DSS 27 26 25 24 23

Sue first named her dog Spike.

But Spike seemed unlike the puppy. So Sue named him Max.

Max did puppy things. He chewed on Dad's old boots. Max could unlace them!

Max could unwind rolls of paper. Sue had to clean up after Max. He was so untidy!

But Max was smart. He could untie a bow on a box. He could hide in the box too.

When Max hid in a basket, Sue was unable to find him. Sue hunted all over!

As Max grew, he seemed afraid of cats. He disliked bugs, too.

In the yard, Max did not run out. Even if the gate was unlocked, Max stayed by Sue.

"Max is smart not to run out. He thinks it might be unsafe," Dad said.

But Sue felt sad. Max just sat and barked at unknown things. Was Max afraid?

Max acted strange on walks. He looked at each person or dog that passed.

Did Max distrust them?

Sue, Max, and her pals played in the backyard. The kids did not know the gate was unlocked.

Max chased the ball, but stopped.

He looked unhappy. He started barking and ran to the gate.

Then Sue saw that the gate was open. Max chased two big dogs away! Her dog was unafraid!

Dad said, "Max was always unafraid, Sue. He just wanted to keep you and your pals safe. He always will."